T0196984

PRAYING THE GOSPEL THROUGH THE ROSARY

A MEDITATION GUIDE FOR EXPERIENCING THE LIFE OF CHRIST AND GLORY OF FAITH THROUGH THE MYSTERIES OF THE ROSARY

JIM KRUPKA

WESTBOW
PRESS®
A DIVISION OF THOMAS NELSON
& ZONDERVAN

WestBow Press books may be ordered through booksellers or by contacting:

WestBow Press
A Division of Thomas Nelson & Zondervan
1663 Liberty Drive
Bloomington, IN 47403
www.westbowpress.com
844-714-3454

ISBN: 978-1-6642-8002-1 (sc)
ISBN: 978-1-6642-8001-4 (e)

Print information available on the last page.

WestBow Press rev. date: 01/12/2023

CONTENTS

INTRODUCTION

The Rosary is a beautiful Scripture-based prayer. But the scripture basis is not apparent to someone without knowledge of the Rosary. Non-Catholics observing recitation of the Rosary hear repeated prayers said quickly. They listen to words praising Mary with little direct attention to Jesus or God the Father. They might notice a few words mentioning a "mystery" but get no apparent focus on what the Mystery is. I understand the lack of connection. What they are missing is the Gospel connection.

Scripture is core to Catholic life. The words of the Gospel are Good News that drive us to live as we do. The world is different because Jesus came and gave us a new covenant of love. This covenant takes more than one. Jesus gave us the Good News, but we must hear it and live it. With the Gospel in mind, the Rosary is a powerful way to keep the Good News before us. To guide us in praying the Rosary, the Church gives us twenty Mysteries that focus on the key events of Jesus' life. The Mysteries begin with the Angel bringing the news of Jesus coming culminating in his Proclamation of the Kingdom and the Eucharist. When meditation on the Mysteries is a part of our Rosary prayer, Jesus is the focus. We gain an ever-deeper friendship with Jesus through meditation on the Gospel. This is something that excites all Christians

The Rosary is a prayer for our time. Sometimes people see the Catholic Church as static and unchanging, with devotions frozen in time. Tradition holds that St. Dominic (d. 1221) devised the Rosary as we know it. The structure of the Rosary evolved between the 12th and 15th centuries. By the 16th century, the form of the five-decade Rosary was in place. Also entrenched in tradition were three sets of mysteries: Joyful, Sorrowful and Glorious. In 2002, Pope John Paul II wrote his Apostolic Letter, *Rosarium*

Virginis Mariae, announcing the addition of the Luminous Mysteries. He referred to them as the Mysteries of Light.

In our modern era, Archbishop Fulton Sheen said, "The Rosary is the book of the blind, where souls see and there enact the greatest drama of love the world has ever known; it is the book of the simple, which initiates them into mysteries and knowledge more satisfying than the education of other men; it is the book of the aged, whose eyes close upon the shadow of this world, and open on the substance of the next. The power of the Rosary is beyond description." He was describing praying the Gospel through the Rosary. The connection happens through meditation on the Mysteries.

The prayers of the Rosary come directly from Scripture. As we pray the Rosary, we begin with the *Apostles' Creed*, which summarizes the great truths of the Gospel. The *Lord's Prayer,* directly from the Gospels, introduces each Mystery. The first part of the *Hail Mary* is the Angel's words announcing Christ's birth and Elizabeth's greeting to Mary from Luke's Gospel. The *Glory Be* is from the Trinitarian blessing at the end of Matthew's Gospel. We are praying the Gospel!

Beyond the prayers are the Mysteries. The twenty Mysteries are highlights from the Gospels. The familiarity and routine of the prayers give us the mental space to contemplate the Mysteries. Through prayers and meditation, our life in Christ will grow richer. That's why we have the Rosary.

As you use this book, don't rush. Use the words about each Mystery to guide your meditation. At the end of each Mystery, there is room to jot down any special thoughts that emerge from your meditation. Let your love for Jesus grow through your Rosary prayer.

How to pray the Rosary

Most people reading this book are familiar with how to pray the Rosary. However, if the Rosary is new to you, the United States Conference of Catholic Bishops (USCCB) give us an overview of how to pray the Rosary. More detail, including the words of the prayers, can be found in pamphlets freely offered in most Catholic Churches as well as print and online resources.

The basic steps given by the USCCB are:

1. Make the Sign of the Cross.
2. Holding the Rosary Crucifix, say the *Apostles' Creed.*
3. On the first bead, say an *Our Father.*
4. Say one *Hail Mary* on each of the next three beads.
5. Say the *Glory Be*
6. For each of the five decades, announce the *(Gospel)* Mystery *(and meditate on the Scripture),* then say the *Our Father.*
7. While fingering each of the ten beads of the decade, next say ten *Hail Marys* while meditating on the Mystery. Then say a *Glory Be.*
8. After finishing each decade, some say the following prayer requested by the Blessed Virgin Mary at Fatima: *O my Jesus, forgive us our sins, save us from the fires of hell; lead all souls to Heaven, especially those who have most need of your mercy.*
9. After saying the five decades, say the *Hail, Holy Queen,* followed by this dialogue and prayer:
10. Verse: *Pray for us, O holy Mother of God.*
11. Response: *That we may be made worthy of the promises of Christ.*
12. Let us pray: *O God, whose Only Begotten Son, by his life, Death, and Resurrection, has purchased for us the rewards of eternal life, grant, we beseech thee, that while meditating on these Mysteries of the most holy Rosary of the Blessed Virgin Mary, we may imitate what they contain and obtain what they promise, through the same Christ our Lord. Amen.*
13. Conclude the Rosary with the Sign of the Cross.

Notice that step 6 encourages us to bring Scripture into our Rosary prayer. The reflection on Scripture brings the Rosary to a level beyond memorized prayers. The Gospel connection should not be missed.

Mysteries for the Days of the Week

The **Five Joyful Mysteries** are prayed on Mondays, Saturdays, and Sundays during Advent.

1. The Annunciation
2. The Visitation
3. The Nativity
4. The Presentation
5. The Finding of Jesus in the Temple

The **Five Sorrowful Mysteries** are prayed on Tuesdays, Fridays, and Sundays during Lent.

1. The Agony in the Garden
2. The Scourging at the Pillar
3. The Crowning with Thorns
4. The Carrying of the Cross
5. The Crucifixion and Death

The **Five Glorious Mysteries** are prayed on Wednesdays and, outside the seasons of Advent and Lent, on Sundays.

1. The Resurrection
2. The Ascension
3. The Decent of the Holy Spirit
4. The Assumption
5. The Crowning of Our Lady Queen of Heaven

The **Five Luminous Mysteries** are prayed on Thursdays.

1. The Baptism of Jesus
2. The Wedding at Cana
3. Proclamation of the Kingdom
4. Transfiguration
5. Institution of the Eucharist

Joyful
Mysteries

Joyful Mysteries

The Joyful Mysteries of the Rosary draw from the Gospel of Luke. They announce and remember the Incarnation. The Joyful Mysteries cause us to meditate on how and why God took human form to live among us. The five Joyful Mysteries are:

The First Joyful Mystery: The Annunciation.

The Second Joyful Mystery: The Visitation.

The Third Joyful Mystery: The Nativity.

The Fourth Joyful Mystery: The Presentation.

The Fifth Joyful Mystery: Finding of Jesus in the Temple.

FIRST JOYFUL MYSTERY: THE ANNUNCIATION

Most Catholics know the content and order of the prayers of the Rosary. But there is so much more. Taken in total, the twenty Mysteries of the Rosary give us a guided meditation on the entirety of the Gospels. The Gospel connection lets the Rosary become more than a series of devout prayers. It reflects on Jesus among us as a necessary part of God's eternal plan.

Reflecting on the First Joyful Mystery, the Annunciation, consider how this event fits God's plan. As the Angel speaks to Mary, the Gospel of Luke reads, "Behold, you will conceive in your womb and bear a son, and you shall name him Jesus. He will be great and will be called Son of the Most High, and the Lord God will give him the throne of David his Father, and he will rule over the house of Jacob forever, and of his Kingdom there will be no end." (Lk 1:31-33). "Annunciation" is a fancy way of saying "announcement."

In my Bible, there are nearly 1,000 pages in the Old Testament. That is a lot of faith history. As we get to the Gospels, Luke's in particular, a question worth asking is: What was this announcement about, and why did it happen after all those years of covenant faith? We often consider Mary's response to the announcement when we think of the Annunciation. That's important, but how did this fit into God's eternal plan? What other parts around that "announcement" were also part of that plan? On reflection, all of the Old Testament history led to this announcement. The Jewish people were chosen and shaped to open the door to bring all humanity back to

God. A woman was chosen to be conceived immaculately without sin to be the means for God to become one of us. Almost simultaneously, a herald was born to announce the coming of the Lord. The Annunciation was not a one-off event. It is part of God's eternal plan revealed in the Gospels.

As you pray this Mystery, think about how the Annunciation set the platform for the rest of the Gospel. Think about how Jesus's coming into humanity was vital to God's continued covenant of love with us.

Your thoughts?

Second Joyful Mystery: The Visitation

It's simple to pray the Rosary, but not always easy to meditate on the Mysteries. When the Rosary is said at a funeral home or before mass, the pace is usually rapid without much time and quiet space to ponder the Mysteries. As we consider the Joyful Mysteries, the Visitation is an event described in a few words, but mediation offers more. In the Visitation, Mary visits her relatives, Zechariah and Elizabeth. "When Elizabeth heard Mary's greeting, the child leaped in her womb. And Elizabeth was filled with the Holy Spirit and exclaimed with a loud cry, 'Blessed are you among women, and blessed is the fruit of your womb.'" (Luke 1:42). We see Mary as the Ark of the New Covenant, embodying our Lord.

We look to the Old Testament and King David as we ponder the Visitation. The Ark of the Covenant contained the Law of Moses, the staff of Aaron, and the heavenly manna. The faith-filled people of David's time knew that the Ark was the dwelling place of the Lord. When we understand the context of David and the Ark, the details of the Visitation take on more meaning. Consider Elizabeth's words: "Blessed are you among women, and blessed is the fruit of your womb. And why has this happened to me, that the mother of my Lord comes to me?" Elizabeth's words reveal Mary's child as "Lord." Think about how similar these words are to words from David, "How can the ark of the Lord come to me?" (2 Samuel 6:9). David realized that the Ark's presence was a blessing and that God looked kindly on those who properly revered it. Consider also John the Baptist. Though unborn, he leaps in his mother's womb. This single moment sets John's life. His mission in God's plan was to prepare the way of the Lord.

We gain additional vision into God's plan with this second of the twenty Mysteries. Like the Annunciation, the Visitation occurred at a time and place necessary and anticipated far before it happened. The Visitation makes sense in the context of the Annunciation that preceded it and the events after it beginning with the Nativity.

Your Thoughts?

THIRD JOYFUL MYSTERY: THE NATIVITY

———— ✺ ————

The Third Joyful Mystery, the Nativity, is arguably the mystery of Mysteries. Why did God choose to come in such a simple form? As St. Paul tells us, "he emptied himself, taking the form of a slave, coming in human likeness." (Phil 2:7). Many meditations idealize the Nativity like a nativity scene. We get those pictures from the Gospels of Matthew and Luke. Matthew 2:1-12 describes the extraordinary impact of Jesus' coming telling of King Herod's fear and the Wise Men's visit. Luke 2:1-20 emphasizes the simplicity of the Nativity with birth in a stable and presence of shepherds.

The other two Gospels give a deeper foundation for considering where the Nativity fits into God's eternal plan. Mark's Gospel starts with the anticipation of the coming of the Messiah and the role of John the Baptist. He does not include Nativity details. Mark skips ahead to the adult Jesus at his Baptism. John does not give us details of the Nativity either. John provides the theological foundation for the Nativity. John opens with the truth of Jesus as the Word existing from the beginning as one with God. (John 1:1-2) Then he says, "And the Word became flesh and made his dwelling among us." (John 1:14).

As we pray the Rosary, making time for meditation on the Third Joyful Mystery lets us connect our Old Testament faith to the Good News of the Gospels. Why did God take on human form? Why did he start at conception rather than come with the impact of a "ready to deliver" prophet in obvious glory? Meditation on the question includes thinking about what it means to be human and why God would want and need to be part of it. The answer begins with our human need for salvation and God's promise to give it to us. As the Old Testament shows, man could not save himself from sin. However, man does have an active need to be part of atonement for sin. In his infinite wisdom, God became man by doing what man could not do alone. Jesus, the God-man, was able to make satisfaction because all his actions had infinite worth. Yet, humanity was part of it through the Incarnation.

Take time to read the opening chapters of each Gospel and let that feed your meditation next time you pray the Joyful Mysteries.

Your Thoughts?

Fourth Joyful Mystery: The Presentation

Living true to Jewish Law, Mary and Joseph went to Jerusalem to present their firstborn Son to God. The Fourth Joyful Mystery calls us to ponder the meaning of this ritual presentation. Luke is the only Gospel writer to mention the Presentation. For Luke, the Presentation was important. In the first sentence of Luke's Gospel, he tells us what he is doing. He says that he decided to "write an orderly account" (Lk 1:3) of the "events that have been fulfilled among us." (Lk 1:1). Key here is the word "fulfilled." Connection to Jewish faith history was important to him.

Luke's description of the trip to the Temple (Lk 2:22-38) is filled with meaning. First, we see that Jesus was born to a family devoutly Jewish. As they presented Jesus at the Temple, they were living Jewish law that required all firstborn males to be designated as holy to the Lord. There is nothing unusual so far. Any good Jewish parents would do the same. But Luke gives us more. When the Holy Family arrived at the Temple, a man named Simeon met them. Simeon was a devout man. God promised him that he would not die until he had seen the Savior. Simeon reached out to Jesus and spoke prophetic words about the infant. He also warned Mary that she would experience sorrow. A sword would pierce her soul.

As we meditate on the Presentation, we can begin to imagine the life of Jesus. From this day at the Temple, we only have one other detail about Jesus' next thirty years in the Gospels. We can conclude that those years were a genuine experience of humanity. Neither the Gospel writers nor secular historians have anything to say about Jesus' life as a boy or young man beyond his Temple appearance at age twelve.

Worth reflection is some attempt to comprehend the how and why that Jesus, the Son of God, took on our humanity and entered our condition. The "ordinariness" of his first thirty years makes it understandable that Jesus identifies entirely with us.

Also, think about what it means to be devout. Despite all the wonder of the Annunciation and Visitation, Mary and Joseph were "amazed" by Simeon's witness. We do not hear Mary's reaction or Joseph's. This mix of joy and worry in the realm of the unknown future is something very human that we all share.

YOUR THOUGHTS?

FIFTH JOYFUL MYSTERY: FINDING JESUS IN THE TEMPLE

From his infancy until Jesus' Baptism around the age of thirty, the Gospels give us only one event from Jesus' life. For some, this absence of information on the Savior of the World is a mystery, while for others, it is enlightening. The story unfolds in Luke 2:42-52: "After they had completed its days, as they were returning, the boy Jesus remained behind in Jerusalem, but his parents did not know it. Thinking that he was in the caravan, they journeyed for a day and looked for him among their relatives and acquaintances, but not finding him, they returned to Jerusalem to look for him."

At the age of twelve, Jesus traveled with the Holy Family to Jerusalem according to Jewish custom for a festival. Luke is the only evangelist to give us this detail that shows, as in the Presentation, that Jesus was a good Jewish boy in a devout Jewish family. We can also discern that his family was part of a close-knit community. Think about it. Joseph and Mary traveled for three days in perfect comfort that Jesus was somewhere in the caravan with friends and family. As a parent reading this story, I boil with emotions like, how could this boy, incapable of sin, give his parents so much anxiety? Did not those loving and perfect parents notice his absence? Mysteries!

Mary says, "Son, why have you done this to us? Your Father and I have been looking for you with great anxiety." Jesus gives a somewhat smart response, "Why were you looking for me? Did you not know that I must be in my Father's house?" This seems a little like a modern teenager giving a very human response to a parent's question.

Luke goes on to bring more mystery for mediation. "They found him in the Temple, sitting in the midst of the teachers, listening to them and asking them questions, and all who heard him were astounded at his understanding and his answers." A point to ponder here is how much the infinitely wise Jesus knew and how genuine was his human learning. Luke gives us words to say that Jesus, like any human, learned through life. "And Jesus advanced [in] wisdom and age and favor before God and man." This is a mystery. St. Ambrose, a fourth-century teacher in the Church, describes this event as the start of Jesus' public ministry. What Jesus said and did for his next eighteen years remains a mystery.

YOUR THOUGHTS?

Luminous

Mysteries

LUMINOUS MYSTERIES

In meditating on the Luminous Mysteries, we focus on critical events during Jesus' earthly ministry that give us a window into who he was. These are the only Rosary Mysteries that focus on the public life of Jesus. Pope John Paul II said it is important to add these Mysteries to the history of the Rosary because there was a gap between the childhood of Jesus that is meditated upon during the Joyful Mysteries and the suffering and death of Jesus that is meditated upon during the Sorrowful Mysteries.

It is fitting to call these the "Mysteries of Light" because they cause us to pray on Gospel passages that reveal Jesus as human and divine. Exposed is the great mystery of faith of Jesus' Incarnation, leading to his gift of the Kingdom and presence in the Eucharist. The Luminous Mysteries are:

First Luminous Mystery: The Baptism of Jesus.

Second Luminous Mystery: The Wedding at Cana.

Third Luminous Mystery: Proclamation of the Kingdom.

Fourth Luminous Mystery: Transfiguration.

Fifth Luminous Mystery: Institution of the Eucharist.

First Luminous Mystery: The Baptism of the Lord

$$\text{---} \sim \text{---}$$

Each Luminous Mystery reveals a different aspect of Jesus' mission in the world. They highlight his divine origin and nature. Meditation on the First Luminous Mystery, the Baptism of the Lord, begins with reading what we know about Jesus' Baptism drawn from Matthew 3:13-17. We can start our meditation with why Jesus needed to be baptized in the first place. If Baptism is the initiation into the Body of Christ, why was it necessary for the divine embodiment of Christ to go through this ritual? Even John the Baptist tried to prevent him, saying, "I need to be baptized by you, and yet you are coming to me?"

Baptism is the beginning of our spiritual and community life in Christ. We celebrate Baptism in Church, out in the open. The community sees the newly baptized entering the faith-filled community regardless of age. As a community, the words of the rite carry this public sense as we express great joy as we welcome the new member. Jesus was around thirty years old when baptized. People knew him as the carpenter's son, but there was little notice beyond that. His Baptism changed that. He went public. The Baptism of the Lord reveals Jesus as the "Son of the Father." The Gospel of Matthew reads, "After Jesus was baptized, he came up from the water and behold, the heavens were opened [for him], and he saw the Spirit of God descending like a dove and coming upon him. And a voice came from the heavens, saying, "This is my beloved Son, with whom I am well pleased." God the Father is who sends him.

Like us, Jesus submits to a way of life. At our Baptism, we begin a mission of Christian living through our own words or the words of our parents and godparents. We begin a path toward our salvation and the salvation of those around us. Jesus started his saving mission with Baptism at the Jordan. As Jesus came to be one of us, he experienced many things about being human. One of them was Baptism.

As we meditate on this Mystery, the Catechism says, "The baptism of Jesus is on his part the acceptance and inauguration of his mission as God's Suffering Servant" (CCC,536). He is submitting entirely to his Father's will. Christians must go down into the water with Jesus to rise with him. Meditate on how we can be Christlike and submit entirely to the Father's will.

Your thoughts?

Second Luminous Mystery: The Wedding at Cana

———— ⌒⌒ ————

The Second Luminous Mystery, the Wedding at Cana, gives us Jesus' first miracle. In the context of Jesus' miracles, it is mysterious why he chose this occasion to reveal his divine power. Jesus' miracles usually involve healing and things as powerful as bringing someone back to life.

Mary and Jesus were at a wedding in a part of Galilee called Cana. Mary went to Jesus and told him they had no wine. Such an event is quite embarrassing. Jesus responded, "Woman, what is that to me and to you? My hour is not yet come." Mary did not respond. Instead, she went to the waiters and told them, "Do whatever He tells you." Jesus instructed the servants to fill large jars with water. They obeyed and were amazed to find that the water had turned into wine. The evangelist John says Jesus' first miracle "manifested his glory, and his disciples believed in him." (John 2:11).

Miracles are extraordinary signs that accompany the preaching of the Good News. The early part of John's Gospel is referred to as the "Book of Signs." John brings a series of miracles to build and strengthen faith in Jesus. In the miracle at Cana, we see an act of power and kindness. As John tells the story of the wedding at Cana, he begins unveiling Jesus as the Savior of humanity. The other Gospels do not give us this Cana account. But John, writing later than the others, uses this event to methodically provide an understanding of Jesus as fully human and divine. We see the human Jesus as a compassionate man who loved his mother and acted to help others. We see the divine Jesus as one with the power to act beyond the usual order, able to comfort and cure, even cure embarrassment.

As you meditate on this Mystery, think about how things don't always make sense within the limits of our human minds. With wonders before us, let go to faith and see miracles in our days. We can find God in ordinary things. The things of everyday life can become extraordinary when we see God's action in them. As our faith grows, we see miracles before they happen. Mary saw that in Jesus at Cana. For the disciples, seeing this miracle solidified a faith that was already a work in progress.

Your Thoughts?

Third Luminous Mystery: The Proclamation of the Kingdom

⁓

The Third Luminous Mystery, the Proclamation of the Kingdom, is unlike other Rosary mysteries. Rather than a single event, it is an ongoing process that began through the words of the Prophets. Jesus' announcing that the Kingdom of God was here raised the proclamation to a new level. Mark says, "The time is fulfilled, and the kingdom of God is at hand; repent, and believe in the gospel" (Mk 1:15). Like the prophets who came before, the voice of the Lord commands, look to God. Our Catechism says, "Everyone is called to enter the Kingdom. First announced to the children of Israel, this messianic kingdom is intended to accept men of all nations" (CCC, 543).

The proclamation is a thread that continues throughout the Gospels and beyond. Peter's preaching after the Resurrection and Paul's conversion both announce the Kingdom. But what is the Kingdom? In Biblical times kings were common. The Jewish people actively sought a king who would rule in the form of the great and benevolent Kings David and Solomon. The Gospels say, "The Kingdom of heaven is like a treasure buried in a field, which a person finds and hides again, and out of joy goes and sells all that he has and buys that field. Again, the Kingdom of heaven is like a merchant searching for fine pearls. When he finds a pearl of great price, he goes and sells all that he has and buys it." (Matthew 13:44-46).

In most earthly kingdoms, a person is born into the Kingdom. They inherit the rights and burdens as subjects. Within the Kingdom proclaimed by Christ, there is an election. We choose Baptism on our own or through others who promise to nurture us as faithful followers of Christ the King. As we elect to live in the Kingdom, we undergo conversion. In that conversion, we choose to see our life through the eyes of God. We look for a new style of life. Pope Benedict XVI said, "conversion is humility in entrusting oneself to the love of the other, a love that becomes the measure and the criteria of my own life."

As we meditate, how completely am I willing to be subject to God? What is preventing me from loving God and choosing the Kingdom? In this democratic society, can I fully let go of my wish to have things my way and become fully subject to Christ as King?

YOUR THOUGHTS?

Fourth Luminous Mystery: The Transfiguration

The Fourth Luminous Mystery, the Transfiguration, continues unveiling Jesus' human and divine nature. As Pope John Paul II announced the addition of the five Luminous Mysteries, he called them the mysteries of light. The Transfiguration is a profound mystery of light told in three Gospels (Matt. 17:1-13; Mark 9:3-13; Luke 9:28-36).

Just before the Transfiguration (Matthew 16:15), Jesus challenges his disciples, "Who do people say that the Son of Man is?" The Transfiguration opened eyes to see Jesus' nature. Even though he had just fed the masses, the disciples seemed to lack a sense of wonder and awe. While Jesus' miracles probably amazed them initially, we do not read of ongoing awe in the disciples' words. Think about how the Transfiguration changed that attitude. "Jesus took Peter, James, and John and led them up a high mountain apart by themselves. And he was transfigured before them, and his clothes became dazzling white, such as no fuller on earth could bleach them. Then Elijah appeared to them along with Moses, and they were conversing with Jesus." (Mark 9:2-4).

With this event, wonder and awe reappear in the disciples. Peter said to Jesus, "Lord, it is good that we are here. If you wish, I will make three tents here, one for you, one for Moses, and one for Elijah." (Matthew 17:4). "While he was still speaking, behold, a bright cloud cast a shadow over them, then from the cloud came a voice that said, "This is my beloved Son, with whom I am well pleased; listen to him." (Matthew 17:5).

Think about how much we are like the disciples. Our faith sometimes becomes routine. We hear the same Gospel words cycle after cycle. For long-term Catholics, the Gospel words are not new news. That brings a human challenge. When we let the Gospel become routine, we lose the sense of awe and wonder that leads us to see how good the "Good News" is. The Transfiguration showed Christ's divinity to Peter, James and John. Their witness, through the Gospels, gives us that same enlightenment. We see the glory of God in the face of Christ. We get a glimpse of what resurrection and eternal life means.

This can bring another challenge. The three apostles did not understand that they could not stay on the mountain. When we have a profoundly spiritual experience, we want to stay there but are usually called back to ordinary life. Our challenge is to keep that awe and wonder alive within the reality of our everyday life. Meditate on how to do that.

YOUR THOUGHTS?

Fifth Luminous Mystery: Institution of the Eucharist

Pope St. John Paul II said that each of the Luminous Mysteries is "a revelation of the Kingdom now present in the very person of Jesus." The Institution of the Holy Eucharist could be the ultimate Mystery. In the Fifth Luminous Mystery, Jesus "took bread, and blessed, and broke it, and gave it to the disciples and said, 'Take, eat; this is my body'" (Mt 26:26).

The Eucharist is God's answer to our spiritual hunger. It is food that feeds the soul. The Eucharist is both material food and spiritual food. St. Thomas Aquinas said, "Material food first changes into the one who eats it, and then, as a consequence, restores to him lost strength and increases his vitality. Spiritual food, on the other hand, changes the person who eats it into itself. Thus, the effect proper to this Sacrament is the conversion of a man into Christ so that he may no longer live, but Christ lives in him; consequently, it has the double effect of restoring the spiritual strength he had lost by his sins and defects, and of increasing the strength of his virtues."

As we meditate on this Mystery, we will be at an intimate place in our faith journey. The Institution of the Eucharist is the last Luminous mediation. We ponder the culmination of Jesus' coming and Passion, bringing us his continued presence in the Eucharist. The Eucharist will remain with the Church until the end of time.

As we meditate on the words of the Gospel, Jesus proclaims, "I am the living bread that came down from heaven; whoever eats this bread will live forever; and the bread that I will give is my flesh for the life of the world."

(John 6:51). It is a truth and Mystery of our faith that the Host that we eat and the Precious Blood that we drink are the Body and Blood of Christ.

Not everyone can see this with the same clarity. It remains a mystery to many who struggle to see the physical presence of Jesus in the Eucharist. They cannot fully understand how the transformed bread they see is truly the Body of Christ. It is a mystery! If you struggle, you are not alone. Keep meditating on the Gospel and praying for the gift of faith. You will move from mystery to faith and into light.

Your thoughts?

Sorrowful Mysteries

THE SORROWFUL MYSTERIES

As we pray the Sorrowful Mysteries, we meditate on Jesus' Passion. These meditations are Good Friday moments, all drawing from the Gospels of Palm Sunday and Good Friday. Unlike the other Mysteries, the Sorrowful Mysteries bring us to focus on one multi-day event: the events of and immediately before the Passion of our Lord.

The First Sorrowful Mystery: Agony in the Garden.

The Second Sorrowful Mystery: Scourging at the Pillar.

The Third Sorrowful Mystery: Crowning with Thorns.

The Fourth Sorrowful Mystery: Carrying of the Cross.

The Fifth Sorrowful Mystery: Crucifixion and Death.

The Bishops of the United States remind us that as we meditate on the Sorrowful Mysteries, we "turn to the Lord, who knows our suffering and longs to give us his comfort and peace. Yet it was our infirmities that he bore, our sufferings that he endured." (Isaiah 53:4). Our challenge in meditating on the Sorrowful Mysteries is that taken literally, the events of the Passion are intense and remote to our modern experiences. But when we take the time to meditate, we can find a connection to our suffering.

First Sorrowful Mystery: The Agony in the Garden

────── ∿ ──────

The First Sorrowful Mystery, the Agony in the Garden, is an intimate moment with Jesus. He is alone and full of human emotion. "Then Jesus came with them to a place called Gethsemane, and he said to his disciples, "Sit here while I go over there and pray." He took along Peter and the two sons of Zebedee, and began to feel sorrow and distress. Then he said to them, "My soul is sorrowful even to death. Remain here and keep watch with me." He advanced a little and fell prostrate in prayer, saying, "My Father, if it is possible, let this cup pass from me; yet, not as I will, but as you will." When he returned to his disciples, he found them asleep." (Mt 26:36-40).

Matthew captures Jesus' thoughts and prayers just before his arrest. He prayed for strength and deliverance. In earlier Gospel passages, Jesus describes his suffering and death. Having given the disciples a preview of the Passion, imagine his pain when he found them asleep. We know that in the depth of that sad night, Jesus again said "yes" to his Father.

The Agony in the Garden becomes real in our times of desperate need. I know some reading this have faced the prospect of intense suffering and impending death. I know others know what it is like to be alone at a dark moment. Meditating on this Mystery unites God and Man through Jesus and our human experiences.

This Mystery forces us to focus on prayer and what comes from it. I heard a mother who lost a daughter in an accident say, "I believe in miracles, but I don't know who gets them." Jesus prayed so hard that he was sweating blood, but he did not get a way out of suffering from those prayers. After his arrest, Jesus seems to get the peace that carries forward in his calm interaction with Pilate. Eventually, we hear him say words of understanding of the purpose of it all when on the Cross, he says, "It is finished." (John 19:30).

As we meditate, let's ask, how deeply do we lay our souls before God as we pray? Are we open to an answer from God that is not exactly as we ask? Can we find peace letting go to God?

YOUR THOUGHTS?

SECOND SORROWFUL MYSTERY: SCOURGING AT THE PILLAR

In the Gospels, we read that Pilate recognized Jesus' innocence. Pilate hoped to satisfy the crowd by whipping Jesus, then letting him go. We know the crowd did not accept that and pressured Pilate to execute Jesus. So, in Jesus' case, scourging was not a means of punishment on its own. Whipping was a preliminary step in the process of execution. Historians tell us that flogging was part of most Roman executions. Scourging happened with a short whip with weights to add force. The man was stripped and tied to a post. The scourging was intended to weaken the victim to near collapse.

The Gospel of John tells us how the scourging transpired. "Then Pilate took Jesus and scourged him. And the soldiers plaited a crown of thorns, and put it on his head, and arrayed him in a purple robe; they came up to him, saying, 'Hail, King of the Jews!' and struck him with their hands" (Jn 19:1-3). St. Teresa of Avila wrote, "I saw an image representing Christ sorely wounded, and so conducive was it to devotion that when I looked at it, I was deeply moved to see Him thus, so well did it picture what He suffered for us. So great was my distress when I thought how ill I had repaid Him for those wounds that I felt as if my heart were breaking, and I threw myself down beside Him, shedding floods of tears and begging Him to give me strength once for all so that I might not offend Him."

In our meditation, a focus can be on why did Jesus allow this to happen? Scourging is a historical fact. Roman and Jewish records document that the Crucifixion occurred. The Mystery is the "why" and "for what purpose." The answer is similar to understanding the Agony in the Garden. In the act of love and obedience to the Father, Jesus said "yes" to this act of redemption. St. Teresa helps us relate and find the purpose. She challenges us to use meditation on Jesus' suffering to amend our lives. She says, "If You, Lord, are willing to suffer all this for me, what am I suffering for You? What have I to complain of? I am ashamed, Lord, when I see You in such a plight, and if in any way I can imitate You, I will suffer all trials that come to me and count them as a great blessing."

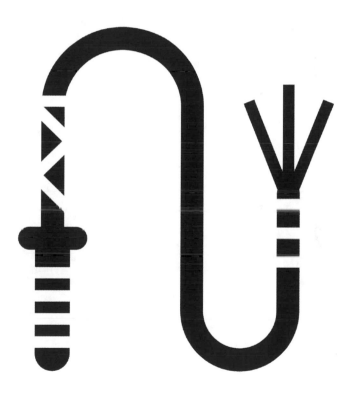

YOUR THOUGHTS?

Third Sorrowful Mystery:
The Crowning with Thorns

To be crowned with thorns is not only to feel physical pain but also to suffer humiliation. The Mysteries of the Scourging, Carrying of the Cross, and Crucifixion include elements of what would have been a typical Roman crucifixion. The men executed with Jesus likely experienced those steps. Scourging and the Cross were instruments designed to bring on death. Crowning with thorns was different and unique to Jesus.

Scripture tells us what happened. "Then the soldiers of the governor took Jesus into the praetorium, and they gathered the whole battalion before him. And they stripped him and put a scarlet robe upon him, and plaiting a crown of thorns they put it on his head, and put a reed in his right hand. And kneeling before him they mocked him, saying, 'Hail, King of the Jews!'" (Mt 27:27-29). Three of the four Gospels record this event (all but Luke). In John's Gospel, Pilate presented Jesus to the crowd one more time while wearing the crown of thorns. The crowds again rejected Jesus and called for His Crucifixion.

As we meditate on this Mystery, focus on the intentional humiliation aimed at Jesus. The crowning of thorns tells us much about Jesus. His witness to who he was before Pilate set the stage for the soldiers to add humiliation to Jesus' pain. Consider his continued silence in the face of the soldiers' abuse. Our Church tells us, "It is love 'to the end' (Jn 13:1) that confers on Christ's sacrifice its value as redemption and reparation, as atonement and satisfaction. He knew and loved us all when he offered his life" (CCC, 616).

Looking at humanity, even today, it is easy to see how those with power have the capacity to add insult to injury. Whether it is a war crime or bully, abusive boss, parent, or spouse, humiliation often multiplies the suffering of the weak. One with power can mock and belittle to advance their power or simply as sport over a victim.

Meditate on Pilate's actions, Jesus' appearance, and the crowd's response. Look deep to see whether you add insult to injury in pride-filled moments when dealing with others. According to St. Thomas Aquinas, pride is "the greatest sin in man," "the beginning of all sin," and "Man's first sin." (Summa Theologiae II-II 161, 6-7; 163, 1). He further tells us that "the root of pride is found to consist in man not being in some way subject to God and His Rule."

Your Thoughts?

Fourth Sorrowful Mystery: Carrying the Cross

——— ⌇ ———

John 19:17 says Jesus carried the Cross himself to Golgotha, or "Place of the Skull." The other Gospels say a man named Simon carried it for him (Luke 23:26, Mark 15:21, Matthew 27:32). "And they compelled a passer-by, Simon of Cyrene, who was coming in from the country, the Father of Alexander and Rufus, to carry his Cross. And they brought him to the place called Golgotha (which means the place of a skull)." (Mk 15:21-22). Our Church reminds us, "By accepting in his human will that the Father's will be done, he accepts his death as redemptive, for 'he himself bore our sins in his body on the tree' (1 Pt 2:24)." (CCC, 612).

Jesus carrying his Cross teaches us about the nature of suffering. Many times suffering does not seem aligned with a loving God. Some good people suffer for years against all sorts of pains. Some find ways to go on with love for God and joy in their hearts. Some give up. Jesus' falling, mentioned three times in his Passion, significantly shows us the difference between perseverance and giving up. Each time Jesus fell, he got back up. From his "agony in the garden," we know his answer to the "why" part of this. He was following God's Will under his own free will choice. For us, as it was for Jesus, sometimes that means freely accepting suffering that comes to us.

This meditation calls us to recognize suffering, weakness and falling as part of life. It is also a mysterious part of God's plan. Many of our human emotions confront us as we ponder this Mystery. Why does this or that happen to me? Why does it feel like God abandoned me when I try so hard to follow him? What compromises in faithful discipleship do I make for my comfort rather than following God's Will?

The U.S. Council of Catholic Bishops gives us a pair of prayer intentions as we ponder this Mystery. First, we should pray for "all who labor under burdens that seem too great to bear—due to illness, age, poverty, cruelty or injustice—that our prayers and aid will lighten their crosses." Second, we should remember those "who struggle to live the Gospel of Life, that they might pick up their crosses and walk the way of sorrows with the Savior of the world." These prayer intentions are as much for ourselves as for others. We ask God for strength as we ask that he give strength to others.

Your Thoughts?

Fifth Sorrowful Mystery: The Crucifixion

An emotional connection to the Crucifixion is not easy. As we meditate on this Mystery, we need to move from our world today to the reality of the Crucifixion. That's why taking time to meditate on this Fifth Sorrowful Mystery is important. We miss much if we announce it and move on. One tool over the last millennium to help this spiritual connection is art. Many great paintings, sculptures, music, and poetry were created for the churches of Europe. A traveler to Rome will find masterpieces in churches and museums. Paintings by masters like Caravaggio or Michelangelo belong in churches. They were created to help us get fruit from the mysteries of faith.

From the Gospel of Luke, "And when they came to the place which is called The Skull, there they crucified him, and the criminals, one on the right and one on the left. And Jesus said, 'Father, forgive them; for they know not what they do." "It was now about the sixth hour, and there was darkness over the whole land until the ninth hour, while the sun's light failed; and the curtain of the Temple was torn in two. Then Jesus, crying with a loud voice, said, 'Father, into thy hands I commit my spirit!' And having said this he breathed his last." (Lk 23:33-46).

Pope Benedict XVI, then Cardinal Joseph Ratzinger, described artist Matthias Grünewald's "Crucifixion" as perhaps the most moving depiction of the Crucifixion. It was painted in the early 16th century for a monastery where the monks cared for the sick. The painting was comforting to those suffering from the Plague. They could relate to the wounds in Christ. The artist chose to paint Jesus suffering sores and blisters like those of the

Plague. Church Fathers called this the "admirable exchange." God suffered our pains, so we can be healed and live a new life.

We all experience pains in the course of life. Most are not on the scale of the Plague or wounds of the Crucifixion. By meditation, we can connect with Christ and find some purpose in the difficulties we face. We can also find the strength to find forgiveness from those who have wronged us as Jesus did on the Cross.

A meditation tip: find an image of some great art depicting the Crucifixion. Have it in your prayer book next time you pray the Sorrowful Mysteries. Pause and reflect before moving ahead with the ritual prayers.

Your Thoughts?

Glorious

Mysteries

THE GLORIOUS MYSTERIES

After the somber meditation on the Fifth Sorrowful Mystery, the Crucifixion, beginning to meditate on the Glorious Mysteries, is a true Easter moment. We suddenly face boundless joy after thinking about loss, suffering, and death. We join the women who came to find Jesus' tomb empty. We strive to seek, through meditation, connection to the reality of the Resurrection. It is easy to say the words, but putting ourselves in the event is difficult. The Glorious Mysteries describe the hope and mystery of our faith. This hope of eternal life and unity with Christ is why any suffering we encounter in this life is worth the price.

The Glorious Mysteries guide us to meditate on why we are Christian. The Glorious Mysteries are:

The First Glorious Mystery: The Resurrection.

The Second Glorious Mystery: The Ascension.

The Third Glorious Mystery: Descent of the Holy Spirit.

The Fourth Glorious Mystery: The Assumption.

The Fifth Glorious Mystery: Crowning of Our Lady Queen of Heaven.

First Glorious Mystery:
The Resurrection

Jesus did what he said he would do. He was victorious over the Cross. We know it was not apparent to Jesus' disciples that this would happen even though he told them. They heard the words, but it was a mystery. The First Glorious Mystery presents us with the same challenge. Through Jesus' humanity, he experienced life and death. The combination is easy to comprehend. The intellectual walk into the mysterious comes with the Resurrection. Think about the emotions of those closest to Jesus as they experienced the risen Lord. Luke describes the experience. "But on the first day of the week, at early dawn, they went to the tomb, taking the spices which they had prepared. And they found the stone rolled away from the tomb, but when they went in, they did not find the body. While they were perplexed about this, behold, two men stood by them in dazzling apparel; and as they were frightened and bowed their faces to the ground, the men said to them, 'Why do you seek the living among the dead? He is not here, but has risen'" (Lk 24:1-5).

As we meditate on the Resurrection, part of the challenge is to make this incredible event real. I have a favorite rosary meditation path. It is outdoors and about a third of a mile long. On that path, the Fifth Sorrowful Mystery, the Crucifixion, is in shadows under a clump of trees. On the other side, the meditation spot for the Resurrection is in open sunshine. It takes effort to walk around the trees to find the Resurrection. The women who went to Jesus' tomb had to go through something like this. They went to the tomb and found it empty. An angel gave them the good news. As they took in this news, they began to experience the reality of the Risen Lord. John Paul II wrote, "The contemplation of Christ's face cannot stop at the image of the Crucified One. He is the Risen One." (Novo Millennio Ineunte, #28).

As we meditate on this Mystery, we make our faith genuine. St. Paul and our Catechism say, "'If Christ has not been raised, then our preaching is in vain and your faith is in vain.' (1 Cor 15:14). The Resurrection above all constitutes the confirmation of all Christ's works and teachings." (CCC, 651). Moving from the Crucifixion to the Resurrection means believing in the bridge from this life to Heaven.

Your Thoughts?

SECOND GLORIOUS MYSTERY: THE ASCENSION

⌒⌘⌒

This final event in Jesus' earthly ministry is closely linked to the first. Our faith tells us that he descended from Heaven and became one of us through his Incarnation. As we ponder the Second Glorious Mystery, the Ascension, the Catechism describes this connection. "Only the one who 'came from the Father' can return to the Father: Christ Jesus" (CCC, 661). Mark describes the day. "So then the Lord Jesus, after he had spoken to them, was taken up into heaven, and sat down at the right hand of God." (Mk 16:19). The Ascension was the call to the disciples to get on with the work Jesus commanded them to do. While they were looking at the sky, suddenly, two men dressed in white garments stood beside them. The men said, "Men of Galilee, why are you standing there looking at the sky? This Jesus who has been taken up from you into heaven will return in the same way as you have seen him going into heaven." (Acts 1:10-11).

We recite in the Apostle's Creed: "On the third day he rose again; he ascended into Heaven, he is seated at the right hand of the Father, and he will come again to judge the living and the dead." The last part of this passage is food for thought: the words about judgment. We are reminded that there will be a day when we must account for what we do with our life. We all want to be innocent and virtuous but are imperfectly human. Jesus' Gospel combining judgment with forgiveness is to spur us to become more Christ-like. Understanding that our actions have consequences motivates us to avoid sin. When we take the Gospel truth that God is Love, we can guide our efforts to be closer to Jesus, whom we love. Indeed, we want to avoid sin and the punishment that goes with it. Our meditation on this mystery gets rich when we focus on our ultimate destination as Heaven.

Jesus ascended into Heaven and left us what we need to go home to him. We have the Church and all the daily encouragement and strength we can get from it. Within the Church, we have the Sacrament of Confession. This is our opportunity to do course corrections. We are guided to find God's graces through prayer. We focus on the Lord when we pray, crowding out thoughts that tempt us into sin. Instead, we move to the more Christlike path to eternity with him.

YOUR THOUGHTS?

THIRD GLORIOUS MYSTERY: THE DESCENT OF THE HOLY SPIRIT

———◦✳◦———

At the Last Supper, Jesus promised that he would send the Spirit. He told his disciples, "The Advocate, the Holy Spirit that the Father will send in my name—he will teach you everything and remind you of all that [I] told you." (John 14:26). The disciples needed the strength of the Spirit.

Scripture describes their rapid conversion from a group huddled in fear to a group who boldly went out to bring the world to Christ. The Apostles were properly afraid. They hid in a locked house, fearing they would suffer the same fate as Christ. But soon after the Resurrection, the Spirit came with the force of wind and fire. We read in Acts of the Apostles, "When the day of Pentecost had come, they were all together in one place. And suddenly, a sound came from heaven like the rush of a mighty wind, and it filled all the house where they were sitting. And there appeared to them tongues as of fire, distributed and resting on each one of them. And they were all filled with the Holy Spirit and began to speak in other tongues, as the Spirit gave them utterance." (Acts 2:1-4).

Our Church teaches us that this Spirit is genuinely divine as God. From the Catechism, the "'Holy Spirit is the proper name of the one whom we adore and glorify with the Father and the Son. The Church has received this name from the Lord and professes it in the Baptism of her new children." (CCC, 691).

The Descent of the Spirit had a profound impact on the disciples. When the Spirit came as a strong wind and tongues of fire, the disciples were "filled" with the Holy Spirit. Meditate on what it means to be filled with the Holy Spirit. When we celebrate Confirmation, we believe that the Spirit comes to individuals through the Sacrament. At that moment of Confirmation, we don't see fire or feel strong wind. What do we feel? What did we get at our Confirmation? We believe we get gifts of the Spirit. We list the gifts as wisdom, understanding, knowledge, counsel, fortitude, piety, and fear of the Lord.

Ponder how you experience these gifts in your life. I suspect most of us would say that the Holy Spirit did not come down and make our lives easier in an instant. The world of the Apostles did not instantly change after they received the Spirit either. Most eventually suffered a martyr's death. The real gift of the Holy Spirit is the wisdom and courage to do God's will. Meditate on how to respond to God's will in a more powerful, Spirit-filled way.

Your Thoughts?

Fourth Glorious Mystery:
The Assumption

Mary remained on earth for several years after her Son ascended into Heaven. At the end of her natural life, she was taken, body and soul, into Heaven. The Assumption is a unique mystery to ponder since not all Christians view this event in the same way. Regardless, all can consider what is possible with God. As St. John wrote his second book, known as Revelation or Apocalypse, he describes a woman "who brought forth a male child, one who is to rule all the nations with a rod of iron . . . [the one] caught up to God and his throne." (Rev12:5). This woman is clothed with the sun. In the Assumption, Jesus brings his mother home. John had a uniquely personal relationship with Mary. In John's Gospel, Jesus looks to Mary and the disciple "whom he loved," saying, "Behold your mother." (John 19:27).

Although the Assumption of Mary is not explicitly mentioned in the Scriptures, the Church has held that Mary was assumed into Heaven body and soul for centuries. Our belief in Mary's Assumption grows out of her Immaculate Conception. "Henceforth all generations will call me blessed; for he who is mighty has done great things for me" (Lk 1:48-49).

As Pope Pius XII declared the truth of the Assumption, he reflected on nearly 2000 years of belief that if death and bodily corruption come about because of sin, certainly the sinless one, Mary, would not be subject to such things. In making the proclamation, he said, "For which reason, after we have poured forth prayers of supplication again and again to God, and have invoked the light of the Spirit of Truth, for the glory of Almighty

God who has lavished his special affection upon the Virgin Mary, for the honor of her Son, the immortal King of the Ages and the Victor over sin and death, for the increase of the glory of that same august Mother, and for the joy and exultation of the entire Church; by the authority of our Lord Jesus Christ, of the Blessed Apostles Peter and Paul, and by our own authority, we pronounce, declare, and define it to be a divinely revealed dogma: that the Immaculate Mother of God, the ever Virgin Mary, having completed the course of her earthly life, was assumed body and soul into heavenly glory."

Mary's Assumption offers a foretaste of our anticipated Resurrection of the Body. Meditate on Mary's Assumption in the spirit of hope that someday we will share that heavenly residence.

YOUR THOUGHTS?

Fifth Glorious Mystery: The Crowning of Our Lady Queen of Heaven

Like the Assumption, not all Christians view the Crowning of Mary similarly. That's why it merits the name "mystery" and is worthy of meditation. In Revelation, John describes a woman "caught up to God and his throne." (Rev12:5). "And a great portent appeared in heaven, a woman clothed with the sun, with the moon under her feet, and on her head a crown of twelve stars." (Rev 12:1). This is part of God's ultimate triumph.

Mary certainly played the role of "blessed among women" to bring about the triumph. The Catechism says, "Finally the Immaculate Virgin, preserved free from all stain of original sin, when the course of her earthly life was finished, was taken up body and soul into heavenly glory, and exalted by the Lord as Queen over all things, so that she might be the more fully conformed to her Son, the Lord of lords and conqueror of sin and death." (CCC, 966).

In the Old Testament days, King David's successor, Solomon, reigned with his mother, Bathsheba, at his right hand. In that culture, a Queen Mother would approach her son, the King, to speak on behalf of another person. Queen Mothers in other Near Eastern cultures had the same influence. In Mesopotamia, the Queen Mother was an intercessor for the people. The advocacy role of the Queen Mother did not reduce the King's absolute authority.

St. Ephraim in the Fourth Century said, "After the Mediator (Jesus), you (Mary) are the Mediatrix of the whole world." Church Fathers at Vatican II said, "the Blessed Virgin is invoked in the Church under the titles of Advocate, Helper, Benefactress, and Mediatrix." These roles fit a Queen and Queen Mother. Theologian and scholar Dr. Scott Hahn points out that just as David and Solomon are types of Jesus, the "Son of David," so Mary's role in the Kingdom of the Son of David is prefigured by the role of Queen Mother.

We have the reality of Mary as our Spiritual Mother. The Gospel of John, describing words from Jesus' last breathing moments on the Cross, says, "Woman, behold your son. Then he said to the disciple, Behold your mother." (John 19:26-27). Pope Leo XIII confirmed what had been a long-standing belief. The Pope said that regarding Mary's role as Mother, "Now in John, according to the constant mind of the Church, Christ designated the whole human race."

YOUR Thoughts?

O my Jesus, forgive us our sins, save us from the fires of hell; lead all souls to Heaven, especially those who have most need of your mercy.

Prayer requested by the Blessed Virgin Mary at Fatima

ABOUT THE AUTHOR

Deacon Jim Krupka is an author, clergyman, charity director, business executive, husband and father. His previous works include *Make Your Marriage Unbreakable* and *The Benevolent Edge*. He holds a Master of Theology Degree from Saint Meinrad Seminary. He has over 23 years of service as an ordained Catholic Deacon. Jim currently serves the Diocese of Gaylord, Michigan. He also serves the Diocese of Honolulu, Hawaii, on the island of Molokai. He came to the Gaylord Diocese after four years in the Westminster Diocese of London, United Kingdom. Prior to that, he served the Diocese of Rockford, Illinois. His primary ministry focus is marriage preparation and enrichment.

Over the years he has served in short-term assignments such as assisting Catholic Relief Services during their 2000 strategy renewal as a strategy advisor. He was invited to address the United States Council of Catholic Bishops (USCCB) on the Morality of the Global Economy. He served as President of a network of health clinics dedicated to providing healthcare to the uninsured or underinsured. He served as an officer, director and general campaign chairman for various United Way entities. He is co-founder of a local charity focused on using music to mitigate bullying in schools. Deacon Jim has been a leader in business and industry for nearly fifty years.

He and his wife of 49 years have five grown children and operate a farm in Northern Michigan.

Printed in the United States
by Baker & Taylor Publisher Services